Wood Lathe Projects

For Fun & Profit

Dick Sing

Text written with and
photography by Alison Levie

Schiffer Publishing Ltd

77 Lower Valley Road, Atglen, PA 19310

DEDICATION

DEDICATION

To Cindy my wife, companion, and best friend.
The one who shares and tolerates my many moods
and my ever present dust.

Printed in China
ISBN: 0-88740-675-0

We are interested in hearing from authors with book ideas on related topics.

Published by Schiffer Publishing Ltd.
77 Lower Valley Road
Atglen, PA 19310
Please write for a free catalog.
This book may be purchased from the publisher.
Please include $2.95 postage.
Try your bookstore first.

CONTENTS

CONTENTS

INTRODUCTION

INTRODUCTION

When I bought my first lathe in 1965, a used one, I paid the grand sum of ten dollars. Turning became my favorite pastime. Back then there was not much information available. After 20 years of turning without the aid of instruction or classes, a new door was opened to me. I attended my first demonstration in 1986 and was amazed and humbled at the skill, techniques and artistic innovations being used by others. That is when I decided I needed to learn those skills. I have attended symposiums, demonstrations, and workshops, and taken hands on classes to increase my skills and knowledge of turning. And the more I turn, the more I love it.

Tools I used to be afraid of, I now use with confidence. I now share the skills I learned, by teaching others through demonstrations and personal instruction, at the same time learning more myself through these experiences. Today there are books, videos, classes, symposiums, demonstrations, articles and many other types of information from which to learn. A number of clubs and associations have been formed which can also help broaden your knowledge and give you a chance to meet with other turners to discuss your techniques and problems.

In 1989, when the GM plant where I had been working for 29 years closed, I decided to supple-ment my income by doing art shows. This gave me a chance to sell my work through shows which I enjoy doing. I also get to visit new and different places while making new friends among the people I meet.

My first love is turning bowls and watching each new shape as it emerges. But unfortunately these are not always what sell. I started projects that are described in this book as my "bread and butter" projects. These smaller projects can be done easily and offer the public a variety of gifts from which to choose.

I feel that the wood lathe is the least used tool in most shops; they are used for "catch alls" rather

than the machines they are. The revolving work piece and hand held tools seem to intimidate many people, and if the wood lathe is used improperly, this fear is justified. If used properly however, the lathe can be your friend. I handle and use my tools with a firm but light touch. I find that for every action there is a reaction. The lighter the touch the less severe the reaction if a faux pas is made.

I find that working with a wood lathe is like riding a bicycle. When you become to confident, it will teach you a new trick. Respect and understand it, but do not fear it.

At this time I would like to say something about my beliefs on sharpening tools. There are many books that will tell you how to sharpen your tools. They describe a set way to sharpen, but I find that sharpening styles need to be developed individually to meet each person's needs. The bottom line to remember is to keep your tools sharp. The sharper the tool the cleaner the cut. The cleaner the cut the less you sand, and this makes Dick happy. You also want to sharpen your tools the same way each time: repeatability. Practice will increase repeatability.

Each person also needs to develop their own style for placement of the tool rest and use of the tools. The general rule is that the tool rest should be at the centerline, but this placement is not always possible or desirable. Position the tool rest where you feel comfortable and safe cutting the wood. I have only mentioned tool position when it was important for a particular cut. Otherwise, experiment. Make friends with your lathe and your tools, and work out the relationship that works best for you.

Another area of exploration and fun for the turner is the wood. I enjoy working with different types of wood. I often use logs which I call "found wood." These are logs that I have chanced upon. I find that the experience of cutting open a new log is like when I was young and dating a new woman. You never know what to expect. It can be a treasure or firewood. I use a variety of woods including exotic and fancy woods which I purchase from wood dealers. This allows me access to woods with different colors and grain patterns that cannot be found locally.

The goal of this book is to entice people to turn that storage table into a useful and satisfying tool. As for tools needed in addition to the lathe, I find that I am a tool junkie. I either have, or have tried, most tools and chucks. Knowing that most people do not have these, my projects can be accomplished with basic tools and equipment. This is the time for the KISS Theory. **Keep It Simple Sir!**

In choosing my projects for this book, I have kept them challenging yet enjoyable and safe to do. You will notice in each of my projects that there is room for creativity in the shape of the piece. A beginning turner may want to develop the form by copying someone else's form. The pictures in this book should provide guidance to you if you would like to copy mine. Do not be afraid to develop you own shapes. These examples are all free form. You have to size the piece correctly, but as for the shape, anything goes.

Finally, I would like to say that I am a turner not a writer. I appreciate the opportunity to work with people who could help take my wood turning skills and put them to words for others to share.

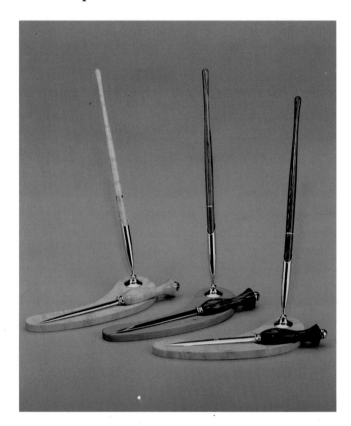

ACKNOWLEDGEMENTS

Craft Supplies U.S.A.
1287 E 1120 S.
Provo Utah 84601
(specialists in woodturning tools)

One good Turn
3 Regal Street
Murray, Utah 84107
(domestic and exotic woods)

The Berea Hardowood Co.
125 Jacqueline Drive
Berea, Ohio 44017
(wood and turning supplies)

The Hardwood Connection
420 Oak Street
DeKalb, Illinois 60115
(wood and supplies)

Woodcuts Ltd
7012 Highway 31
Racine, Wisconsin 53402
(hardwood and carving supplies)

TURNING THE CLOCK

TURNING THE CLOCK

The clock in this demonstration is made from cocobolo which is a Central American rosewood. It was chosen for its vivid color and grain pattern. Some people, including myself, are allergic to the dust. Therefore, I use breathing protection when I work with it. A Racal air helmet works well, but a dust mask will help.

Shear scrape the waste block from the center out with a gouge in order to create a flat surface.

Attach a chuck to the head stock to hold the wood in place. A screw chuck, shown here, is a good choice because it is easy to change. A faceplate can be used instead.

A waste block that has been pre-drilled with a 1/4" hole is screwed onto the chuck or attached to a faceplate with screws.

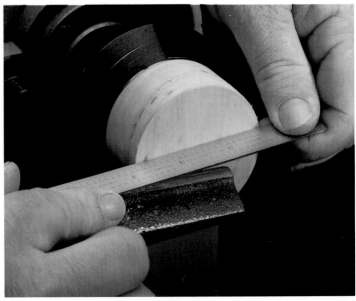

Check for flatness using a straight edge.

With a bandsaw, cut a turning blank approximately, 3" by 3" by 3" (this is a guideline not an exact requirement), for the clock body, and locate the center of the blank with a compass.

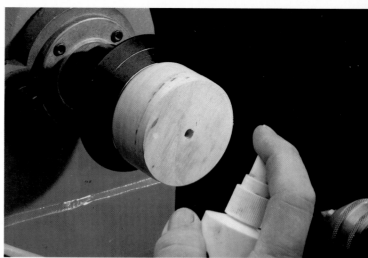

and apply accelerator to the waste block.

Aligning the tail stock with the center of the turning block will help you center it on the waste block.

Join the turning blank to the block, aligning it with the tail stock and tighten to clamp pieces.

Cover the lathe bed with a paper towel or rag for protection. Then apply cyanoacrylate (super) glue to the bottom of the blank...

Run a bead of cyanoacrylate glue around the joint to fill gaps and provide additional strength.

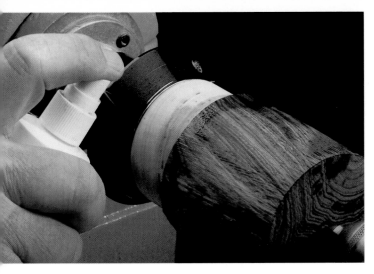

Spray with accelerator.

When the blank is clean...

Clean up the turning blank with the gouge...

face off the front surface, cutting from the outside in towards the center...

making sure that all the imperfections in the wood's surface are removed and that you have a good solid blank with which to work.

The result.

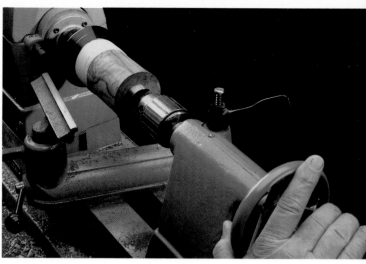

Using the 1/4 inch spindle gouge, mark the center so that you can locate the drill. This is very important. If there is any misalignment between the head stock and the tail stock, establishing a new center on the turning blank will help to align the tail stock to create a hole in the proper position.

Slow the lathe down to the slowest speed and drill by cranking the tail stock into the blank.

Insert a 1 3/8" Forstner drill bit into the tail stock.

Drill to a depth roughly equal to the depth of the bit. Make the hole deep enough so that the instructions for the clock can be placed in the hole behind the clock mechanism.

While the lathe is stopped, locate the point of the bit at the new center and lock the tail stock. This centers the tail stock.

The space for the time piece is made.

Use the 3/8" spindle gouge to establish the general shape of the bezel.

to rough out the basic shape.

After creating a smooth curve in the front, start on the sides...

At this point the final shape has yet to be determined.

reducing them...

With a parting tool, establish a flat surface to seat the watch insert.

Start detailing the face using a 1/4" spindle gouge. Create a cove.

Using a shear scrape, come back across the face, smoothing the surface.

Next to this, cut a bead.

After you have defined the desired detail, finish the main part of the face with a larger gouge -- here I am using a 3/8" spindle gouge.

Reduce the face from the center to the outside to establish a form. Notice that I have removed the seat for the clock mechanism while refining the shape of the face. I will reestablish it later when the shape is defined.

Reestablish the seating surface for the clock mechanism with a parting tool.

To make the bead stand out a little, use a small, well-sharpened, vee point scraper to add a detail line in the groove.

You are ready to sand the bezel. Have sheets of 180, 220, 320, and 400 grit sandpaper in order. Cut the sheets into sixths, and fold each piece into thirds. This makes the sheets easy to hold and creates many edges with which to sand.

The bezel now looks like this when viewed from the front...

and this from the side.

Sand up to an edge, so that all lines remain crisp.

Never hold the sandpaper still.

Keeping the sandpaper in motion reduces the tendency to produce concentric scratches.

Ready for the next step.

Check closely, both visually and with your hands to make sure initial sanding has been done to your satisfaction.

Refine with progressively finer grit sandpaper.

Apply a coat of Deft™ Semi-gloss urethane with a brush to act as a filler.

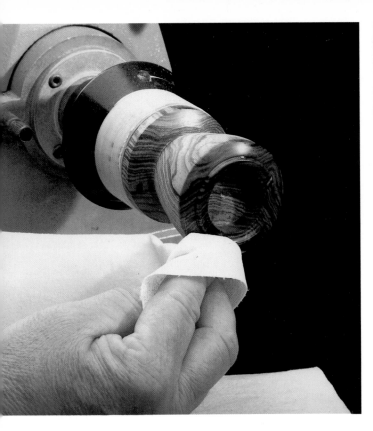

Returning to the back of the clock, reduce the diameter of the turning at the waste block.

Wipe off with a clean paper towel immediately. Shop rags can be used if they are lint free.

Use a parting tool to reduce the diameter at the joint...

Any jar can be used to hold the urethane. I epoxy a brush, with a wooden disk for support, into the lid of a jar. This makes a handy applicator for applying the finish.

until it is released from the waste block.

Free at last.

Measure with the caliper and use a parting tool to set the diameter...

Reduce the size of the waste block to make a jam chuck to hold the clock. You will turn a tenon to fit tightly inside the hole drilled for the clock mechanism. This will allow you to hold and drive the clock body while finishing the back of the clock.

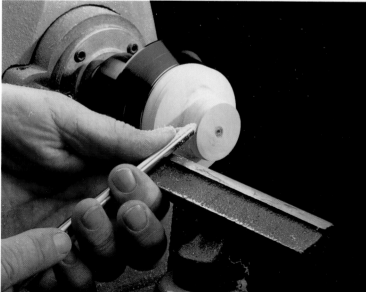

of the tenon.

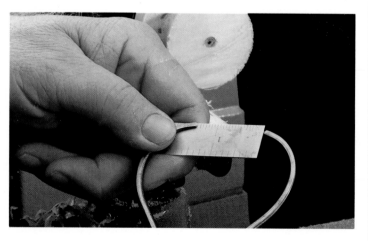

Rough cut the waste block until you get the tenon close to the diameter of the hole. Then set the calipers slightly larger than the diameter of the hole.

The final press fit is established by trial and error.

Reduce and test until it nearly fits.

Then make a slight taper on the leading edge of the tenon.

Face the surface of the tenon, making it flat or slightly concave.

Carefully test the clock on the tenon again. Because the tenon is tapered, the clock should start to go onto the tenon easily, but will hit the tenon when the diameter of the tenon equals that of the clock opening. The clock will leave a mark at this point of interference.

The diameter of the tenon at this rub mark is the exact diameter you are seeking. Now finish turning the tenon by reducing it to the rub mark diameter, working slowly and carefully so you don't remove too much.

If you do remove too much and the fit is too loose, you can wrap a piece of tape around the tenon to create a snug fit.

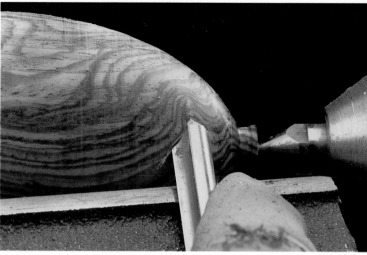

Tip the 3/8" spindle gouge up so that you can use the side of the flute, allowing it to cut like a pocket knife rather than using the point as you would in a normal cut.

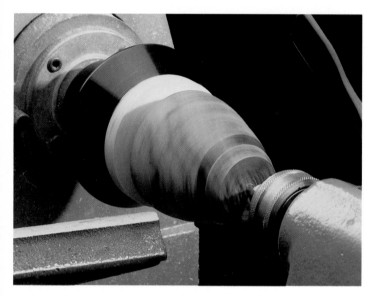

Put the clock body on the tenon. If it is done correctly the body will run true. If it wobbles, check for chips and make sure that it is tight against the tenon. Make necessary adjustments. Move the tail stock up and with the lathe running, allow the tail stock to find its center axis before locking it down. This will minimize any misalignment. The tail stock will apply a little pressure to support the stock and give added confidence while shaping the back of the clock.

Move from the small diameter to the large using light pressure.

Refine the shape of the back using a shear scrape to get a finished surface.

Back the tail stock off so you can finish the tail end of the clock. Use the tip of the gouge to remove the nubbin left for the tail stock support.

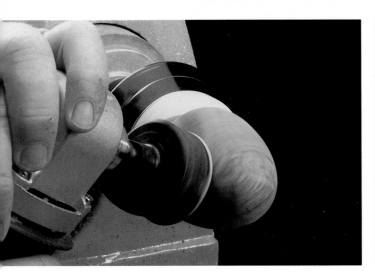

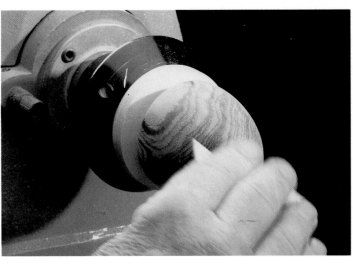

Power sand with a drill in a con-rotating direction -- the opposite direction from the one in which the lathe is running. This process can be done totally by hand, but it is faster with the power sander. Use a velcro backed sanding pad, starting with a 120 grit.

Then sand with the 400 sandpaper in the direction of the grain to eliminate the rings.

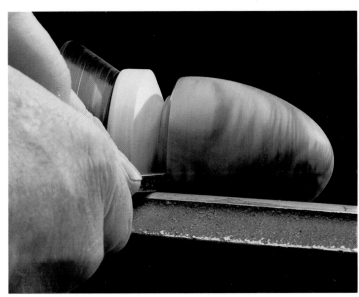

Finish the sanding by hand, using the 180, 220, 320, and 400 grit sandpapers...

Using a vee point scraper, add a fine line on the transition from the face to the body...

as described before.

for decoration and to accentuate the break.

Apply Deft™ to the back section and dry with a paper towel.

Remove the clock body from the tenon and repeat the oiling and buffing on the inside of the mechanism hole as well.

While the lathe is stopped, apply tung oil or another turning oil finish with 0000 steel wool. (I find that finishing with the lathe turning leaves lines.) This scrubs the Deft™ off the surface while leaving it in the pores as a filler, and provides an oiled finish.

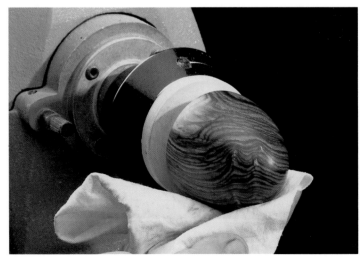

Hand buff, with the lathe off.

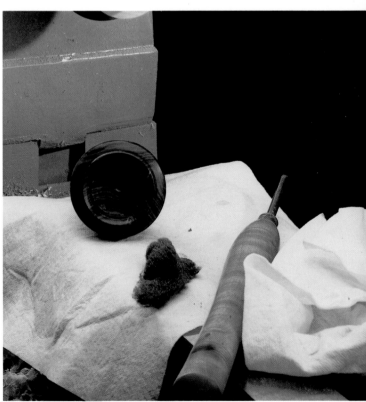

The clock is almost ready to keep time.

Locate the side you want to be the bottom and give it a flat surface with a disk or belt sander. This can also be done with a rasp and sand paper.

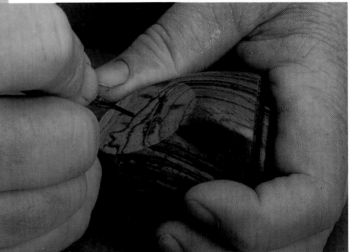

Sign the finished product with a woodwriter or burning tool. You can also use a vibrating engraving tool. Then finish as before with 0000 steel wool and tung oil

Finish off with sandpaper rubbing on a flat surface.

Put the clock insert into the bezel. If you have left room for the instructions, these can be placed behind the clock insert now.

The clock is finished.

THE CANDLE DISH

THE CANDLE DISH

I chose to make this candle dish from Koa, a wood native to Hawaii. This is an attractive, warm colored wood with iridescent qualities, and is one of my wife's favorite woods.

Drill a hole in the blank, approximately 5/8" deep (deep enough to clear your screw so the screw does not bottom out, leaving a space between the surface of the block and the screw chuck.)

Mount the blank on the screw chuck or faceplate.

True the blank.

Start to shape bowl with a 3/8" gouge.

Remove wood...

leaving a 1/4" diameter tenon for relocating the work later.

until you start achieving the desired shape. The exact shape is up to you and the wood.

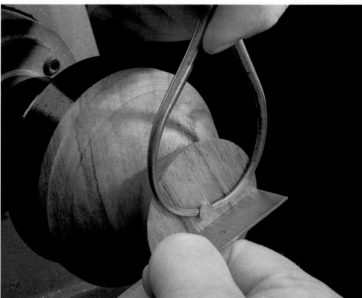

Use the caliper to size the tenon accurately.

Before you have completely finished shaping the bowl, face off the bottom...

Further refine the shape of the bowl.

Put a waste block onto the screw chuck and face it off. When the pilot hole in the waste block is drilled for the screw chuck, it should be 1/4" in diameter, drilled all the way through the block.

The bowl is now shaped like this.

The drilled hole should match the 1/4" tenon on the blank, so that the two can be put together. If you are using a faceplate and waste block, face off the waste block, put a 1/4" drill in the tail stock and drill the pilot hole to match the tenon. Whether you are using the screw chuck or faceplate, you are now ready to put cyanoacrylate glue on the blank and the accelerator on the waste block. Push the two pieces together. Twist and hold together.

A side view. Remove the blank from chuck.

Put the assembly back on lathe.

True the blank and refine the shape.

Use the 3/8" spindle gouge with a shear cut.

Finish shaping the bowl in preparation for sanding.

Turn the inside and create a depression for the globe. Use a 1/4" bowl gouge which has a deeper flute, allowing you to make an inside curve without catching.

To start the cut with a gouge, stand the flute vertical to the bed of the lathe so the point makes an indentation.

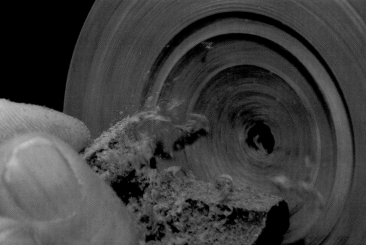

Then roll the gouge into a cutting position and push forward. If this is not done, the gouge will skate across the piece because there is nothing to support the bevel.

Keep cutting...

When the basic shape is roughed out, or if your gouge fouls out, go to a scraper. Position your scraper slightly below the center line. This way if there is a catch, it will knock your scraper away from the surface, rather than having it dig into the wood.

until the bowl form emerges.

Continue to deepen the indentation to fit the candle holder by making successive cuts and regularly testing the depression to check the fit.

When finishing the indentation, leave a little extra room for the globe in case future warping affects the fit.

A good look at the bowl.

Finish the lip with a 1/4" spindle gouge, taking light cuts. I don't care for perpendicular or perfectly square rims, so I always establish an angular surface. Sharp edges are a sign of skilled craftsmanship.

Sand with 120 grit sandpaper and the sanding machine...

inside and out.

Hand sand with 180, 220, 320 and 400 grit sandpaper...

on all sides.

Brush with Deft™ and...

and part the bowl from the waste block.

wipe with a paper towel.

Use medium density fiber board to make a jam chuck to secure the bowl so that the other side can be finished.

Reduce the diameter at the base slightly...

Turn a groove to fit the outer rim of the bowl with a parting tool.

Start with the groove smaller than the diameter of the bowl, and increase the width of the groove until the bowl snaps into the diameter with a tight fit.

If you are worried that the bowl might come off, it can be taped in place.

Proceed slowly and check frequently to see whether the groove is the right size, so the diameter of the groove does not get too large.

Start the lathe and bring the tail stock forward. Let it seek its center and lock the tail stock. The tail stock should apply light pressure to the candle holder.

The bowl snaps into place.

Reduce the foot of the bowl...

to an appealing shape.

Remove nubbin...

Shape the base of the bowl so it balances with the foot.

and begin turning a recess in the foot of the bowl.

Here the indentation is being deepened to achieve a pleasing balance.

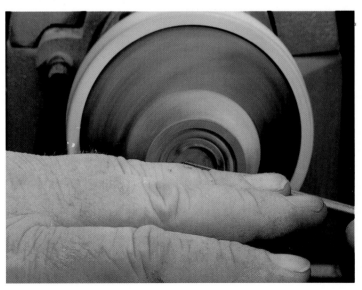

Make the bottom slightly concave.

Sand as before, using 180, 220, 320, and 400.

After you have wiped it dry, the base of the bowl will look like this.

Back to the Deft.

Use 0000 steel wool to oil the candle dish with tung oil or a similar product.

Here is the finished candle dish.

THE DESK SET

THE DESK SET

This project is a variation of the typical pen. I developed this design myself to provide an extra item--something different for my art shows. It makes a very distinctive gift.

For this demonstration, I used a cherry base and Pau Ferro for the pen and letter opener handle. The woods were selected because they contrast very nicely with each other.

For this project, you will need pen and letter opener hardware, a pen funnel and blanks for the letter opener, the wooden base and a pen blank, approximately 5/8" by 5/8" by 10". The hardware can be obtained through many craft supply houses. This particular one calls for 7mm holes. Others may differ slightly. Cut the blank in two with one part as long as the brass tube with a little extra for truing after drilling, and the second part approximately 7 to 8 inches long.

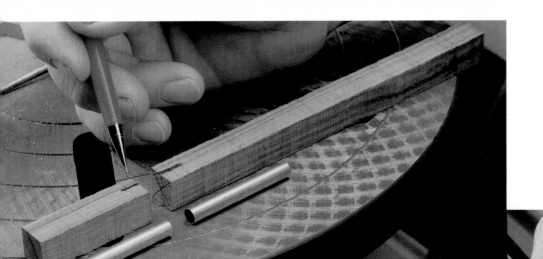

Mark the mating joint with a felt tip pen so you will know later which ends match during assembly.

Using a V-block, position the blank on the drill press so you can drill vertically into the center of the blank.

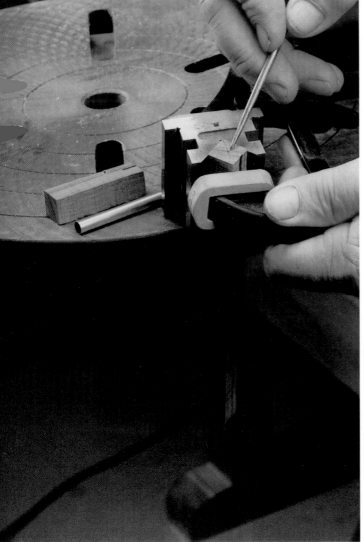

Locate the centers of the joining ends and mark them with an awl.

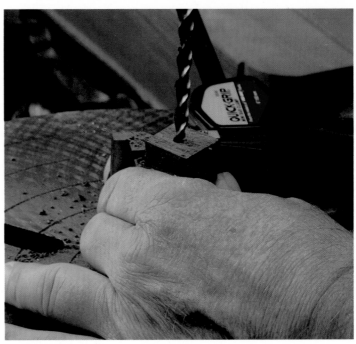

Drill a hole 7mm in diameter. In the short blank this hole needs to be drilled all the way through. In the long blank the hole needs to be the depth of the brass tube.

Cut the blank for the letter opener handle 1/32" longer than the brass tube to allow for truing after drilling. Locate the center of the letter opener handle and drill all the way through.

Cut the base for the desk set on a band saw. You can choose the shape that is most appealing to you. It needs to be about 3/8" thick and 7" long by 3" wide.

Position the brass pen holder fixture on the base.

Mark the spot where the fixture will be attached...

and drill all the way through the base.

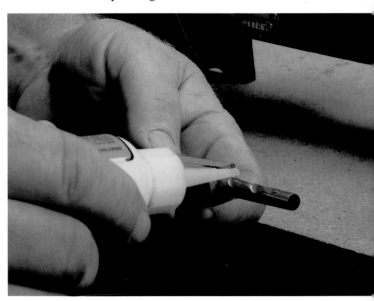

Apply cyanoacrylate glue to the brass tubes and then insert into the handles.

Use a barrel trimmer to square the blank ends to the brass tube. The tool is available where pen supplies are sold.

The tools of the trade for this step.

Use two piece mandrels if you have them. (A mandrel is a tool which is used to hold and drive the assembled blank.)

If you don't have two piece mandrels, you can either purchase them or make them by holding a piece of dowel in a drill chuck. Turn it to fit the inside diameter of the brass barrels. On the tailstock end you can use a 60 degree live center.

Using a skew or gouge, rough turn the blank on the lathe, converting the square peg to a round shape.

Put the shorter pen blank between the mandrels, making sure you know where the marked end is for grain alignment at assembly.

Continue turning...

Test to make sure that the turning is straight by holding a straight edge between the centers on the mandrel shoulders.

until the diameter...

matches the shoulders on the mandrel. (The diameter of the mandrel determines the diameter of the pen.)

While the lathe is turning sand the piece with 180, 220, and 320 sandpaper.

Hand sand with 400 sandpaper in the direction of the grain to eliminate sanding rings.

Apply to the barrel with the lathe running. Move the cloth back and forth so as not to develop pick-up rings from the polish. Continue until a good finish has been built up.

For the final finishing, use a lint free applicator material. Shot gun patches are the perfect size and lint free.

If pick-up rings do develop...

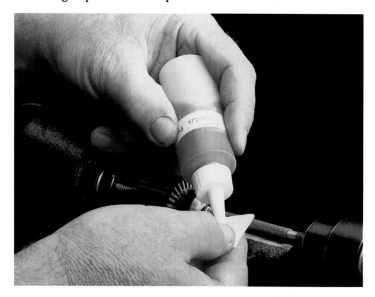

Fold a patch into quarters and pour on a small amount of French polish or friction polish.

use 0000 steel wool to remove them, and refinish as described above.

Re-... the inside so that you can ... assembly.

Notice that I steady the blank with my forefinger. I apply the same pressure with my finger that I apply on the other side with the skew. If this support is not provided, the blank will flex and chatter.

...lank, remove the mandrel ... 0 degree center. Put the blank... and allow the tailstock to find its own center. During ...lling, the drill has a tendency to follow the grain of the blank. By putting the mandrel in the brass tube which is aligned with the hole you drilled, the tail end of the blank is usually thrown off center. Rotate the blank so you can see where the 60 degree center will meet the blank. Align tailstock to this center by moving it slowly to meet the blank in its free state. Allow the tailstock to mark the blank. This is the point you will use for alignment. Lock down your tail stock and apply light pressure.

Make that square peg into a round shape again.

Use a straight edge to test whether the shape is developing evenly. You also must measure how far the brass barrel extends within the blank. The diameter of the the the blank must be maintained beyond the length of the brass barrel before the diameter can be reduced for our design.

I still need to reduce the diameter a little near the mandrel. I have started to shape the other end for a pleasing design.

Using the skew, I always move from the large diameter to small.

Sand with 180, 220, 320, and 400. Again I am using my finger to help support the quill end so that it does not break.

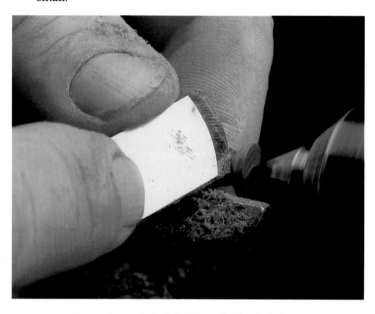

Now I shape the end slightly. I use the heel of the skew to roll over the end, being careful not to cut through.

Hand sanding will remove any rough spots. With the lathe turning, blend that area with the surrounding wood. Continue sanding with the remaining grits.

Thin enough.

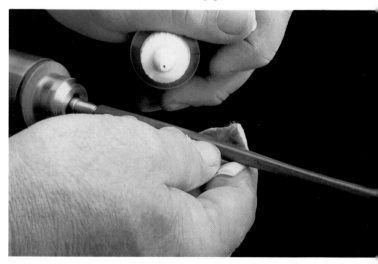

Go back to the polish. If you used steel wool on one part, be sure to use the steel wool on the other part so that the finishes will match.

Tape the pen to the mandrel. When the other end is cut loose from the tail stock, the tape will hold the pen in place.

with the tip of the skew in preparation to part off.

Position the tool rest at the end of the pen, so you can use the skew to part the pen handle from the waste end.

Use the heel or the tip...

Make small vee cuts...

to do the parting.

Support the end with your hand and gently sand, working through the grits of sandpaper.

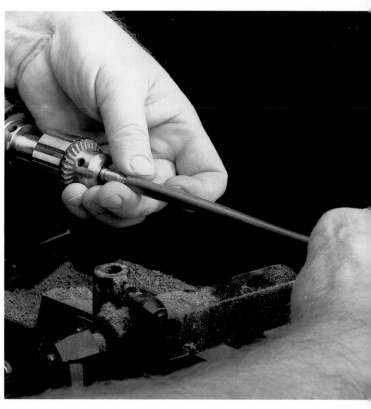

Remove the tape and take the pen off the mandrel, being careful to protect the pen from the point on the 60 degree live center.

Polish the end.

To assemble the pen, note the marked joint for grain alignment, put the tip on the barrel and press it into place with the vise. Make sure the jaws of the vise are wood or are covered with wood so the pen is not marred by the vise.

Insert the twist mechanism by placing the barrel in a pen gauge, a vee grooved block of wood 3 and 7/8" long with both ends squared. This will allow you to seat the twist mechanism without trial and error.

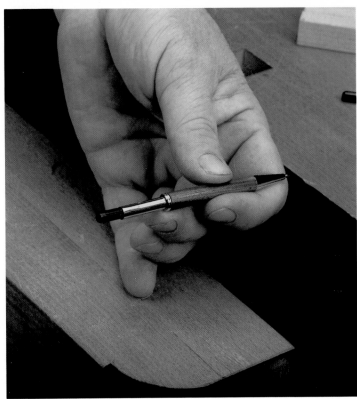

Insert a refill and a center ferrule.

The pen gauge is a hand made vee block device, which helps position the depth of the mechanism so that the refill tip is set in the writing position.

Adjust the pen so it is in the retracted or closed position. Put the long end of the pen onto the twist mechanism, line the grain up with the bottom portion, and push until it is flush with the ferrule.

The finished pen.

Reinstall the two piece mandrel system. Attach the blank for the letter opener handle to the headstock.

Turn the blank to a cylindrical shape. You can use either a skew or a gouge.

Create a shape for the end of the handle using a 3/8" spindle gouge. Start at the large diameter and go in using the normal cut.

then the other.

Continue shaping the handle moving from the larger to the smaller diameter...

Blend the two curves with a light touch...

first from one and...

so that the shape is blended well, no ridge or line.

Sand using the progression of sandpapers, starting with the 180 as described above. Hand sand with the 400 in the direction of the grain, rotating the spindle by hand.

the entire handle, and...

Polish...

attach the handle to the blade.

The finished letter opener.

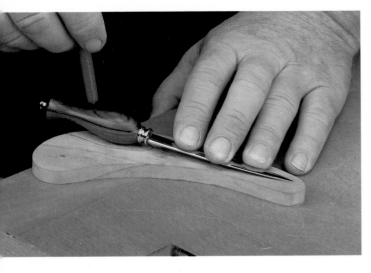

Position the letter opener on the base and trace around its handle including the ferrule. This marked area will allow you to create a depression to fit the handle of the letter opener.

Take light cuts so you do not burn the wood.

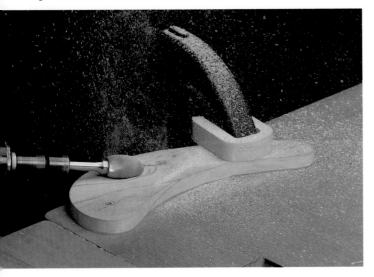

Clamp the base to the bench for stability, and using a die grinder and a burr hollow out the depression. You can also use a chisel or drill and burr.

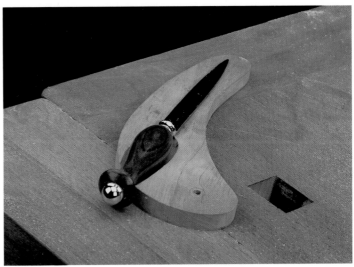

Continue until the depression matches the shape of the handle.

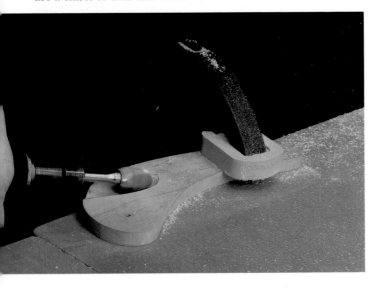

Test fit the letter opener regularly, while continuing to hollow out the depression.

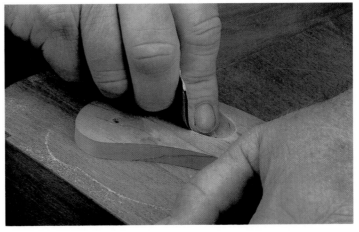

Sand by hand, starting with the depression, which must be finished before the rest of the base can be sanded. As usual, work from the coarsest grain sandpaper to the finest. Final sanding should always be as much with the grain as possible.

Next sand the edges.

Flat sand the surface.

Use tung oil or a similar product to protect and finish the base. Allow the oil to penetrate as called for in the instructions.

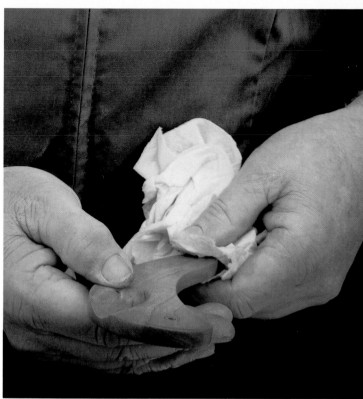

Wipe off. Allow the oil to dry and apply additional coats if desired.

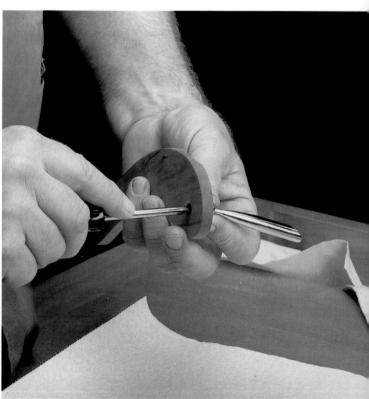

Put the screw in from the backside to attach the funnel.

THE BOOKMARK

THE BOOKMARK

I chose to use Kingwood for this piece because it has bold, contrasting colors, fine grain, and turns easily, which is desirable for such a small piece.

Screw a waste block to the faceplate.

to remove most of the waste.

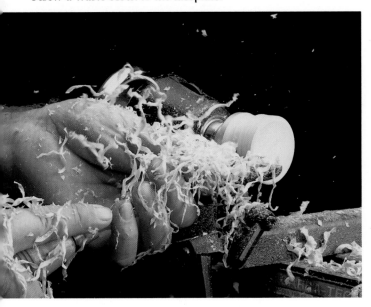

Turn the waste block round by moving evenly back and forth across it with a 3/8" spindle gouge...

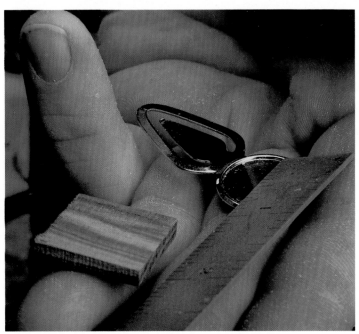

Measure the diameter of the recessed portion of the bookmark. The blank will need to be sized to fit in this recess.

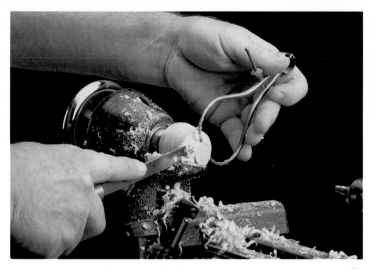

Set calipers to the recess diameter, and using a parting tool, establish the diameter on your waste block.

Apply double-faced tape to the back surface of the blank and center on the tenon.

Using the parting tool, create a small tenon of this diameter. The blank is mounted on this tenon, which because it is smaller than the rest of the waste block, gives room to turn the blank with ease.

Bring up the tail stock, using a flat center or a piece of scrap between the blank and the center you are using to protect the surface of the blank.

Wipe the face of the tenon and the back side of your blank with a piece of tape. This eliminates dust and helps the pieces to stick.

Turn the blank to a cylinder with a 3/8" spindle gouge. Do not turn the diameter smaller than the tenon.

Use a 1/4" spindle gouge to shape the cylinder, creating a domed surface.

until the shape is smooth and creates an even dome.

Start on the outside and move in toward the center with light cuts...

Back off the tailstock..

and lightly turn off the nubbin which will finish shaping the face of the bookmark.

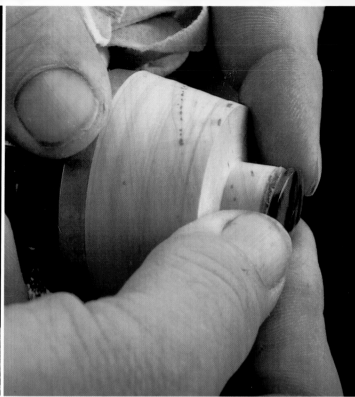

Continue until you build up the finish that you want. Then hold the piece and apply pressure away from the tenon, giving the tape a chance to relax.

Sand using progressively finer grains of sandpaper, starting with 180 and move through 220, 320 and 400. Be careful not to heat the cylinder, because that will make the tape sticky and the piece will start to move. Sand with the 400 by hand. Polish while the lathe is running, with friction polish or

Clean the indentation where the wood will go on the bookmark with a clean paper towel. Decide which direction you would like the grain to run. Apply medium cyanoacrylate glue or silicone adhesive, and align the grain in the direction of your choice.

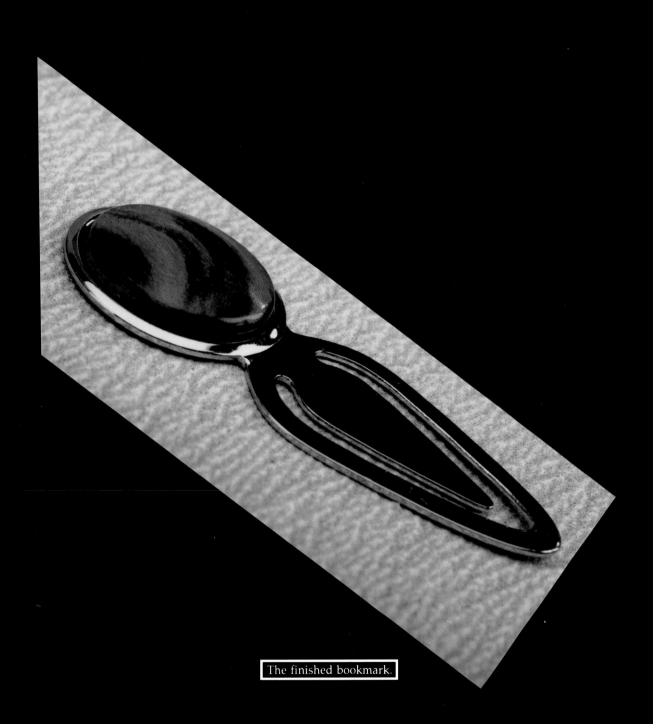

The finished bookmark.

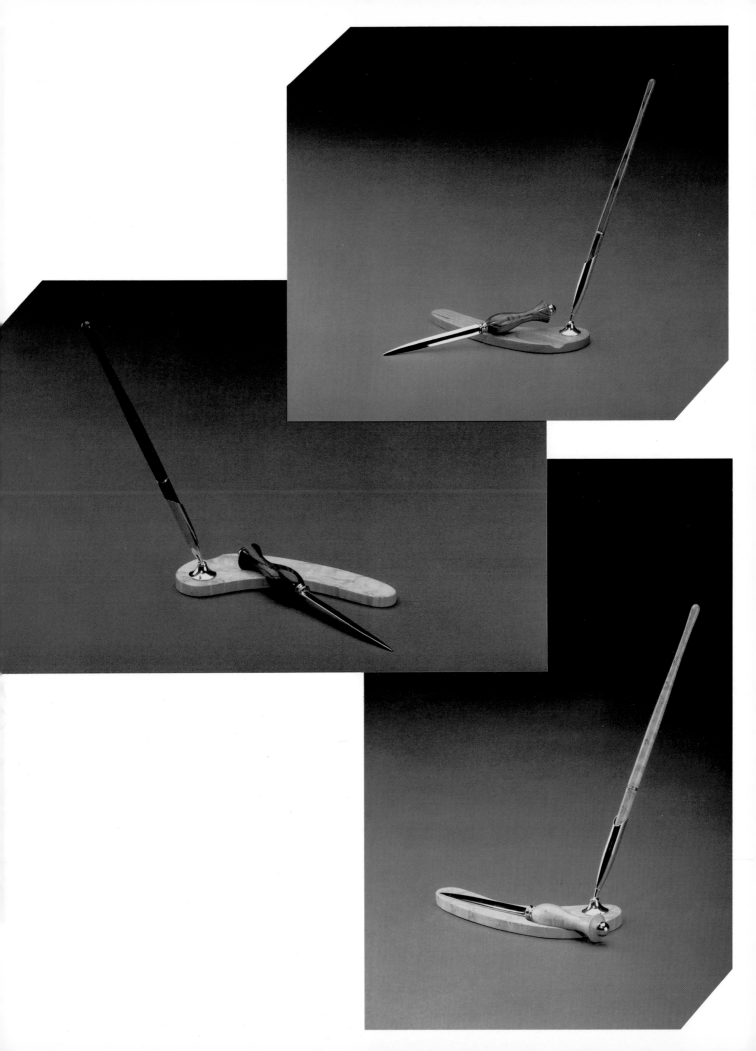

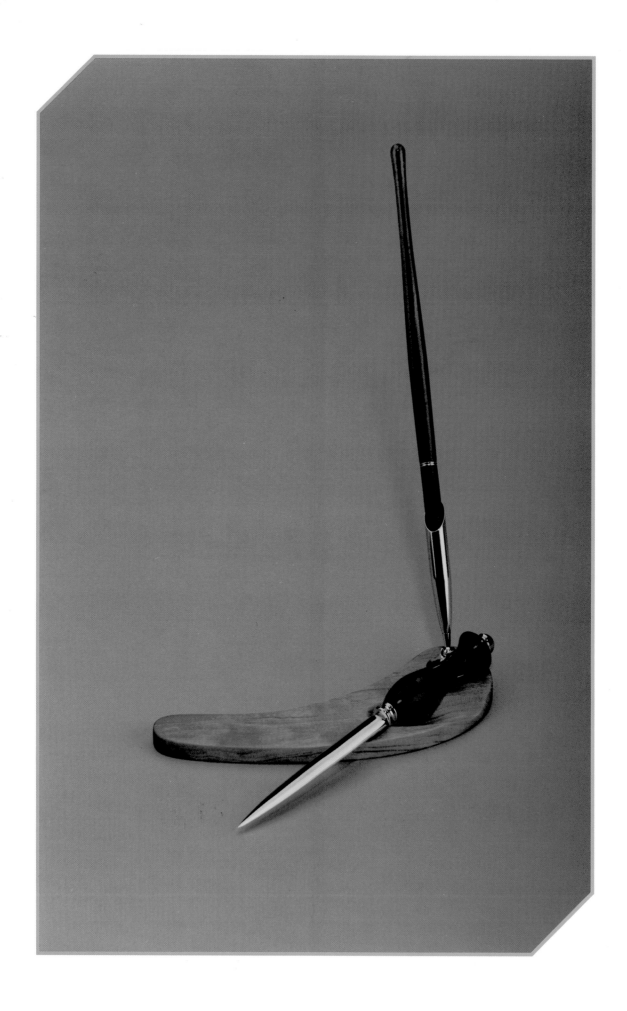

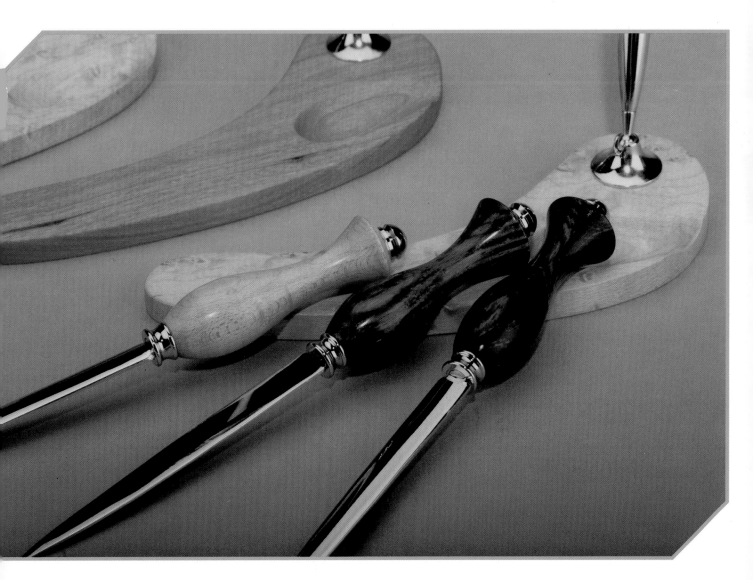